Pacific Spirit

Vancouver

by Karl Herrmann

Layout by Karen Elkins
Production by Bill Ellis
Love and Support Team – Mom and Dad
Inspiration and Support – Austin Scott Herrmann

Images in this book are available as note cards, fine art prints, murals and stock photography. Visit www.karlherrmann.com or www.natureseries.ca

Printed in Canada

Paper Stock: The Sterling Ultra Gloss paper used in this publication is old-growth free, chlorine free and has been harvested utilizing sustainable forestry practices.

Vendor & Distributor Enquiries and Volume Discount Information

If you wish to carry "Pacific Spirit – Vancouver" in your store, distribute it to your current outlets or use the book as a corporate gift, please contact the publisher, Nature Series, at the website www.natureseries.ca.

natureSeries

Cards Books Original Prints

www.natureseries.ca
www.karlherrmann.com

Mixed Sources
Cert no. SW-COC-001271
© 1996 FSC
FSC

"To all dreamers who believe
the impossible is possible."

Karl Herrmann

"There is a road
in the hearts of all of us,
hidden and seldom traveled,
which leads to an unknown
secret place."

Chief Luther Standing Bear

"Wisdom begins with wonder."

Socrates

"Within our dreams
and aspirations
we find our
opportunities."

Sue Ebaugh

"Let the beauty of what you love be what you do."

Rumi

"Little things make big things happen."

John Wooden

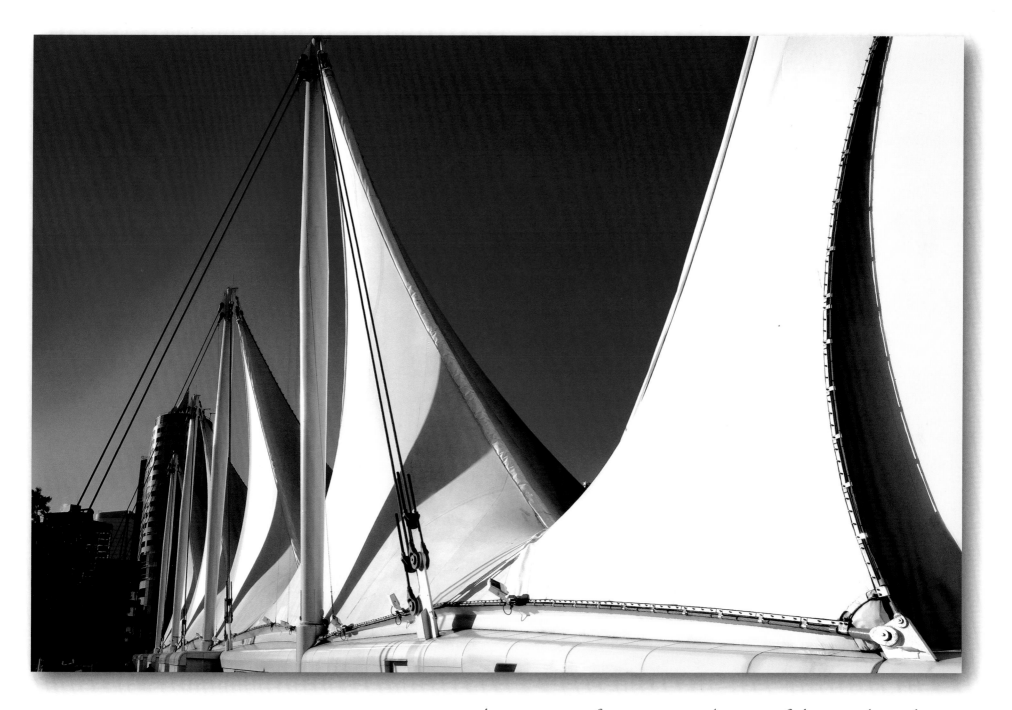

"It is the essence of genius to make use of the simplest ideas."

Charles Peguy

"The man who believes he can do something is probably right, so is the man who believes he can't."

Anonymous

"High achievement always takes place
in the framework of high expectation."

Jack Kinder

"It's never too late to be
what you might have been."

George Eliot

"We will be known by the tracks we leave behind."

Dakota Proverb

"All of our dreams
can come true – if we
have the courage
to pursue them."

Walt Disney

"When you realize there is nothing lacking,
the whole world belongs to you."

Lao-Tzu

"Nothing ever succeeds which exuberant
spirits have not helped to produce."

Nietzsche

"If you refuse to accept anything
but the best, you very often get it."

William Sommerset Maugham

"If the doors of perception
were cleansed, everything
would appear as it is, infinite."

William Blake

"Only those who risk going too far can
possibly find out how far one can go."

T.S. Eliot

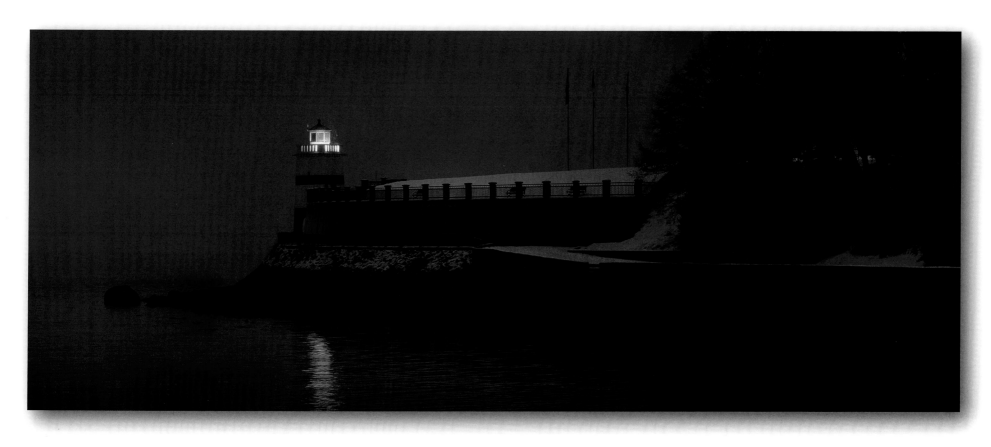

"The man who has no
imagination has no wings."

Muhammed Ali

"The future belongs to those who believe
in the beauty of their dreams."

Eleanor Roosevelt

"For everything you have missed,
you have gained something else."

Ralph Waldo Emerson

"Leap and the net will appear."

Julia Cameron

"Our life is shaped by our mind. We become what we think."

Buddha

"You must do
the things
you think
you cannot do."

Eleanor Roosevelt

"We convince by our presence."

Walt Whitman

"The dictionary is the only place
where success comes before work."

Vince Lombardi

"Only he who keeps his eye fixed on the
far horizon will find his right path."

Dag Hammarskjold

"We know what we are, but
know not what we may be."

William Shakespeare

"Nature is full of genius, full of divinity, so that not a snowflake escapes its fashioning hand."

Henry David Thoreau

"An early morning walk is a
blessing for the whole day."

Henry David Thoreau

"I am always doing things I can't do, that's how I get to do them."

Pablo Picasso

"Remember: If the Creator put
it there, it must be in the right place."

An Indian Chief 1886

"Do it big, do it right
and do it with style."

Fred Astaire

"If you don't have a dream, how ya
make a dream come true?"

Oscar Hammerstein II

"The universe gives to those
who ask without favor."

Walter Russell

"Go confidently in the direction of your
dreams. Live the life you have imagined."

Henry David Thoreau

"Nothing can come between me and
the full prospect of my hopes."

William Shakespeare

"When the student is ready
the master appears."

Buddhist Proverb

"No bird soars too high if he
soars with his own wings."

William Blake

"The possession of anything
begins in the mind."

Bruce Lee

"We must be willing to get rid of the life we've planned
so as to have the life that is waiting for us."

Joseph Campbell

"Give thanks for unknown blessings
already on their way."

Sacred Indian Ritual

"Great men are they who see that spirituality is stronger
than material force, that thoughts rule the world."

Ralph Waldo Emerson

"Fortune befriends the bold."

John Dryden

"Change is the law of life.
And those who look only
to the past or present are
certain to miss the future."

John F. Kennedy

"We do not attract
that which we want,
but that
which we are."

James Allen

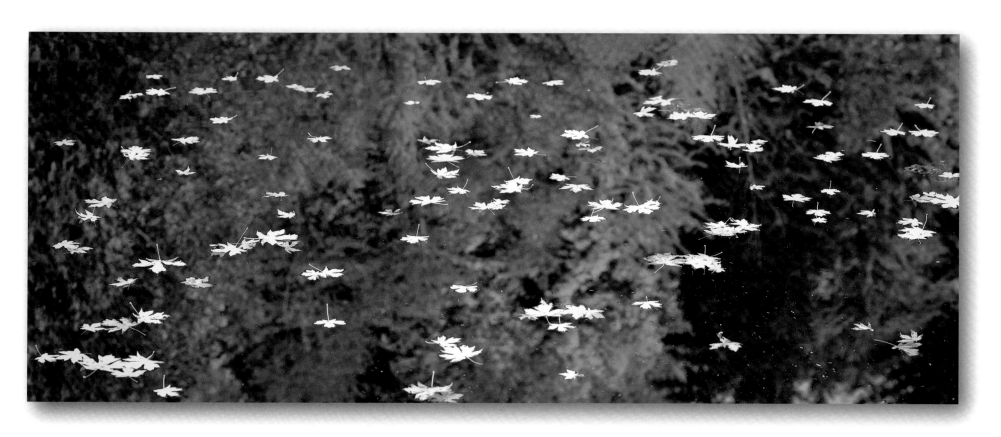

"The only thing necessary for tranquility in the world is that every child grow up happy."

Chief Dan George

"The great thing in the world is not so much where
we stand, as in what direction we are going."

Oliver Wendell Holmes

"Life is what happens when you're busy making other plans."

John Lennon

"They can because they think they can."

Virgil

"Match your strategy
to your skills."

Arnold Palmer

"All great achievements require time."

Maya Angelou

"Yesterday is but today's memory,
and tomorrow is today's dream."

Kahil Gibran

"You will become as small as your controlling desire: as great as your dominant aspiration."

James Allen

"To the mind that is still, the whole universe surrenders."

Lao-Tzu

"Never mistake motion for action."

Ernest Hemmingway

"Humankind has not woven the web of life. We are but one thread within it. Whatever we do to the web, we do to ourselves."

Chief Seattle 1876

"The time is always right, to do the right thing."

Martin Luther King, Jr.

"Nature uses as little as
possible of anything."

Johannes Kepler

"Take time to marvel at
the wonders of life."

Gary W. Fenchuk

"Life is a great bundle
of little things."

Oliver Wendell Holmes

"Great things are achieved by people who believe they will accomplish them."

Warren Bennis

"Action is character."

F. Scott Fitzgerald

"The seed never explains the flower."

Edith Hamilton

POWER

"Dream no small dreams, for they have no power to move the hearts of men."

Johann Wolfgang von Goethe

"Your sacred space is where you find yourself again and again."

Joseph Campbell

"The power of the imagination
makes us infinite."

John Muir

"Success is the ability to go from one failure
to another with no loss of enthusiasm."

Winston Churchill

"Genius seeks regions hitherto unexplored."

Abraham Lincoln

"Nature does nothing without purpose."

Aristotle

"Desire is the presentiment
of our inner abilities, and
the forerunner of our
ultimate accomplishments."

Johann Wolfgang von Goethe

"We do not inherit the earth from our Ancestors,
we borrow it from our children."

Ancient Native Proverb

"A sailor without a destination
cannot hope for favorable winds."

Anonymous

"Dream lofty dreams and as you dream, so shall you become."

James Allen

"Every moment of light
and dark is a miracle."

Walt Whitman

"He conquers who endures."

Persius

"Simplicity is the glory of expression."

Walt Whitman

"There is nothing like a dream
to create the future."

Victor Hugo

"Observe what is with
undivided awareness."

Bruce Lee

"If it can be dreamed, it can be done."

Walt Disney

"The privilege of a lifetime
is being who you are."

Joseph Campbell

"Follow your bliss."

Joseph Campbell

"There are those who travel and
those who are going somewhere."

Mark Caine

"The universe is wider than our view of it."

Henry David Thoreau

"Be still until the sunlight pours through and dispels
the mists – as it surely will. Then act with courage."

Ponca Chief, White Eagle

"Success is getting what you want.
Happiness is wanting what you get."

Carl Hayden

"Joy is not in things, it is in us."

Richard Wagner

"My today is what
I will to make it."

Walter Russell

"He who is outside the door has already
a good part of the journey behind him."

Dutch Proverb

"What we need is more people who
specialize in the impossible."

Theodore Roethke

"The first thing to do in life is to do with
purpose what one proposes to do."

Pablo Casals

"When you cease to dream,
you cease to live."

Malcolm Forbes

"Life is change. Growth is
optional. Choose wisely."

Karen Kaiser Clark

"One touch of nature makes
the whole world kin."

William Shakespeare

"We must be the change
we wish to see."

Mahatma Gandhi

"Give light, and the darkness
will disappear of itself."

Desiderius Erasmus

"True merit is like a river. The deeper
it is the less noise it makes."

Lord Halifax

"In wilderness is the preservation of the world."

Henry David Thoreau

"So many of our dreams seem impossible,
then improbable, then inevitable."

Christopher Reeves

"To every disadvantage there is
a corresponding advantage."

W. Clement Stone

"If you can imagine it,
you can achieve it;
if you can dream it,
you can become it."

William Arthur Ward

"...the unexamined life is not worth living."

Socrates

"Obstacles are those frightful things when you take your eyes off your goals."

Hannah Moore

"Courage is the capacity to
confront what can be imagined."

Leo Rosten

"Heaven is under our feet
as well as over our heads."

Henry David Thoreau

"With ordinary talent and extraordinary
perseverance, all things are attainable."

Sir Thomas Fowell Buxton

"The greatest oak was once a little nut who held his ground."

Author Unknown

"The only way around is through."

Robert Frost

"Nobody ever gave his
best and regretted it."

George Halas

"Go.
Take a walk in nature.
Find a quite place.
Listen to your inner voice.
Fear not.
Follow your voice
and discover
how magnificently
you can fly."

"The greatest architect of the universe never
built a stairway that leads to nowhere."

Robert Millikan

The Photographs